JIM DAVIS

Born: July 28, 1945, in Marion, Indiana.

Grew up: On parents' farm near Fairmount, Indiana.

Brother: Dave (nicknamed Doc).

Parents: Jim and Betty Davis.

Started drawing: When an asthmatic condition forced him to stay indoors.

Graduated: From Ball University with "the lowest accumulative grade point ratio in the history of the university".

Worked: 2 years with an advertising agency, during this time met wife Carolyn, an elementary school teacher.

Comics work: Worked as cartoon assistant for Tom Ryan, creator of TUMBLEWEEDS strip.

In 1978: Created GARFIELD.

In 1982: First GARFIELD TV SPECIAL is released.

In 1986: Created second strip, ORSON'S FARM.

In 1987: Became the third cartoonist in history to have 2,000 newspapers carry his comic strip.

Hobbies: Jim's hobbies include golf, fishing, chess, sandwiches, and good friends, but his favourite pastime is playing with his son, Alex.

ORSON'S FARM

ANNUAL 1991

Created by JIM DAVIS

Written by Gordon Volke

RAVETTE BOOKS

Contents

Published by Ravette Books Limited 1990

Printed and bound for Ravette Books Limited, 3 Glenside Estate, Star Road, Partridge Green, Horsham, West Sussex RH13 8RA by BPCC Paulton Books Limited

ISBN 1 85304 278 1

POWER PIG PULLS IT OFF!

Orson lay dozing in his waller. "What a peaceful place this is," he sighed, looking round the farmyard, "nothing disturbs the quiet calm of the countryside." "Help!" yelled a voice. "The cawing of the rooks, the distant whine of a tractor," continued Orson, "these are the only sounds that break the silence of a summer afternoon." "HELP!" yelled the voice, much louder. "And the occasional voice yelling for help," added Orson, closing his eyes. Then he opened them again. "What am I saying?" he gasped.

Orson leapt out of the waller and raced across the farmyard towards the cries for help. They were coming from Booker. "What's wrong, Booker?" asked Orson, bending down to talk to the young chick. "My roller boots have been taken!" cried Booker. "I left them outside the barn and now they're gone!" Orson wondered what to do for a moment, then he thrust one arm in the air. "This is a job for Power Pig!" he exclaimed.

Orson told Booker to stay where he was while Orson went to put on his Power Pig outfit. He had not gone far when the sound of sobbing reached his ears. Rounding the corner of the henhouse, Orson came upon Wade who was shaking like a jelly. "What's the matter with you?" exclaimed Orson. "Can't you see?" replied Wade. "I'm dripping wet – and you know how much I hate water!" "Did you finally go for a swim, then?" asked Orson. "Of course not!" snapped Wade. "Somebody squirted me with a water-pistol." Instantly, Orson stuck two arms in the air. "Here's a second job for Power Pig!" he cried.

Orson set off to find Booker's roller boots and the person who had squirted Wade with a water-pistol. As he approached the sheep-pens, Orson suddenly lost his footing and fell flat on his back with his legs in the air. As he slithered to a halt, he found himself face-to-face with Lanolin and Bo who were also sprawled out on the farmyard cobbles. "W-W-What happened?" gasped Orson. "Peas!" replied Lanolin. "Peas?" echoed Orson. "Dried peas," explained Bo, indicating the ground all around them, "they're *everywhere*. Someone has split open the sack in the storehouse and is firing them from a pea-shooter."

Orson leapt to his feet. "I wish I had three arms," he cried, "because this is a *third* job for Power Pig!" He tried raising both arms and one foot, but that just made him fall over again. "Never mind all that exclaiming stuff!" snorted Lanolin. "Just get on with action!"

Orson rushed off back to his sty. This time, no-one stopped him on the way and he was able to start rummaging through his wardrobe. "Where IS my Power Pig outfit?" he murmured, throwing a steady stream of clothes over his shoulder. He looked in his chest of drawers, in his Fancy Dress box, in the washing basket – but it was nowhere to be found. Then Orson remembered! "Oh, dear!" he gulped. "What happens now?"

Orson decided to tell the truth. "Listen, you guys," he called, hurrying back towards the others, "I'm afraid I can't solve your problems by being Power Pig." "Why not?" they demanded. "W-W-Well you see," stammered Orson, blushing to the tip of his curly tail, "I sent my suit to the cleaners!"

Booker, Wade, Lanolin and Bo looked at each other indignantly. "Fraud! Con-man! Boaster!" they shouted. Then Booker, who was particularly upset at losing his roller boots, began chasing Orson round the farmyard. The other three joined in. "They're really mad at me," gasped Orson, fleeing round a corner, "I wish I really *was* Power Pig – then I could escape by flying!"

Suddenly, Orson spotted a couple of big balloons bobbing around in the sunshine. There had been a birthday party at the farm the day before and the balloons had been left out as a signal to the arriving guests. The balloons were special gas-filled ones that floated in the air, so Orson snatched them up and tied one to his tail. He held onto the other balloon-string with his hand. Slowly, he felt himself rising into the air. "This is the perfect hiding place," giggled Orson, hovering high above the farmyard, "they'll never think of looking for me up here!"

Orson watched Booker and company searching the farmyard below in vain. He was just wondering how he was going to get down when the problem was solved for him – by a couple of passing birds! Thinking the big red balloons were giant cherries, the birds began pecking at them. BANG! BANG! The balloons burst and Orson found himself plummeting down towards the ground. He braced himself for a painful landing when a familiar figure sneaked out from the farmhouse below. It was Roy. He was wearing roller-boots and carrying a water-pistol in one hand a pea-shooter in the other!

BLAM! Orson landed on top of Roy, flattening him. "Not only have I solved the mystery," chuckled Orson, "I have also caught the culprit!" Booker, Wade, Lanolin and Bo all came running up. They laughed when they saw Roy's flattened form, then they turned to apologise to Orson. "That's okay, fellas," he sniffed, haughtily, "but I don't have to *look* like Power Pig to *act* like Power Pig, you know!" With that, Orson marched off. Then he stopped and turned to his friends again. "Right now, though," he added with a grin, "I want a nice, long soak in the waller. And that's a job for Orson!"

ORSON'S FARM
LOOK OUT, WORLD, HERE COMES...
POWER PIG!
POWER PIG EATS POWER CORN FOR ENERGY, IN ORDER TO PROTECT PIGS EVERYWHERE!
FIRE ONE!
PTOO!
TONK!
United Feature Syndicate, Inc
4-20
POWER PIG WILL NOW DO WHAT HE DOES BEST!
JIM DAVIS
HE WILL MAKE A FOOL OF HIMSELF

HERE'S MUD IN YOUR EYE!
SOMEONE HELP ME DOWN!
HANG TIGHT BOOKER! THIS SOUNDS LIKE A JOB FOR...POWER PIG!
RATS! SHELDON'S IN MY TRUNK
ROY'S IN THE CHICKEN COOP
Z
AND WADE'S BEHIND THE BARN
JIM DAVIS 9-28 © 1986 United Feature Syndicate, Inc.
WHAT HAPPENED TO YOU?
POWER PIG HAD TO SUIT UP IN THE WALLER

POWER PIG RULES, OK?
RUN FOR YOUR LIVES! POWER PIG IS ON THE RAMPAGE!
HEE HEE
WHAT A JERK
© 1986 United Feature Syndicate, Inc.
RUN FOR YOUR LIFE! POWER PIG IS ON THE RAMPAGE!
AAACK! HELP! HELP!
I CAN ALWAYS COUNT ON GOOD OLD WADE
JIM DAVIS 9-14

Lanolin's Letter Puzzle

Put the first letter of each picture in its box to spell the names of 6 farm animals.
When you have solved the puzzle, can you spot the odd one out?
(Here's a clue to help you: 'Take care not to bark up the wrong tree!')

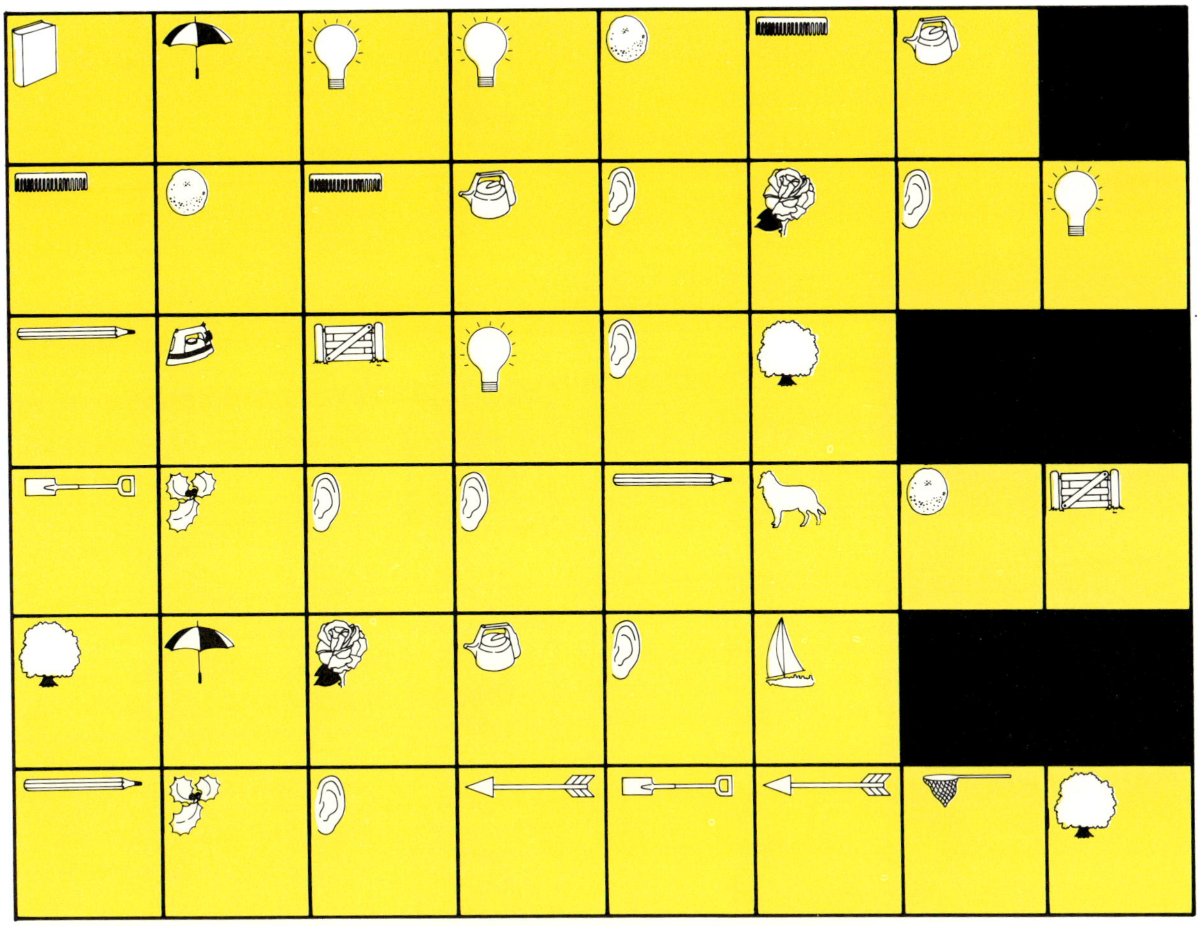

Answers

B	U	L	L	O	C	K	
C	O	C	K	E	R	E	L
P	I	G	L	E	T		
S	H	E	E	P	D	O	G
T	U	R	K	E	Y		
P	H	E	A	S	A	N	T

SHEEPDOG is the odd one out.
(He lives and works with the farmer; the other animals are kept on the farm as livestock.)

ORSON'S STORYTIME QUIZ

Orson is a great reader and loves telling stories to his friends. He is particularly fond of children's stories and has set 10 questions to see if your knowledge of famous fairy tales is equal to his.

1

Cinderella
When the Fairy Godmother is getting Cinderella ready for the ball, she waves her magic wand at a pumpkin. What does it turn into?

2

Snow White
Can you complete this sentence?
'When the Wicked Queen looked in the mirror, she always asked the same question:
"Mirror, mirror, on the wall,
---'s --- ------- --
---- ---?" '

3

Sleeping Beauty
For how many years did the beautiful Princess sleep?

(a) 1 year
(b) 10 years
(c) 100 years
(d) 1,000 years

4

The Ugly Duckling
How did the Ugly Duckling discover that he had turned into a swan?

5

The Little Tin Soldier
Who was the Little Tin Soldier in love with?

6

Jack And The Beanstalk
Where was Jack going when he exchanged the cow for the handful of beans?
(a) To market
(b) To visit the King
(c) To London to seek his fortune

7 **Hansel And Gretel**

The children were attracted to the Wicked Witch's cottage because it was made of money.

(a) True?
(b) False?

8 **The Pied Piper**

Why did The Pied Piper lure all the children away from the city of Hamelin, never to return?

9 **King Midas**

Can you complete this sentence?
'Everything King Midas touched turned to – – – –.'

10 **Goldilocks And The Three Bears**

Who did the middle-sized bed, middle-sized chair and middle-sized plate of porridge belong to?

(a) Mother Bear
(b) Father Bear
(c) Baby Bear

Answers

1. A beautiful carriage
2. Who's the fairest of them all
3. (c) 100 years
4. He looked at his reflection in the lake
5. The ballerina
6. (a) To market
7. (b) False. Because it was made of cake and sweets
8. Because the Mayor refused to pay him for getting rid of the rats
9. Gold
10. (a) Mother Bear

IF YOU THINK THIS IS CORNY, WAIT TILL YOU HEAR THE JOKES!

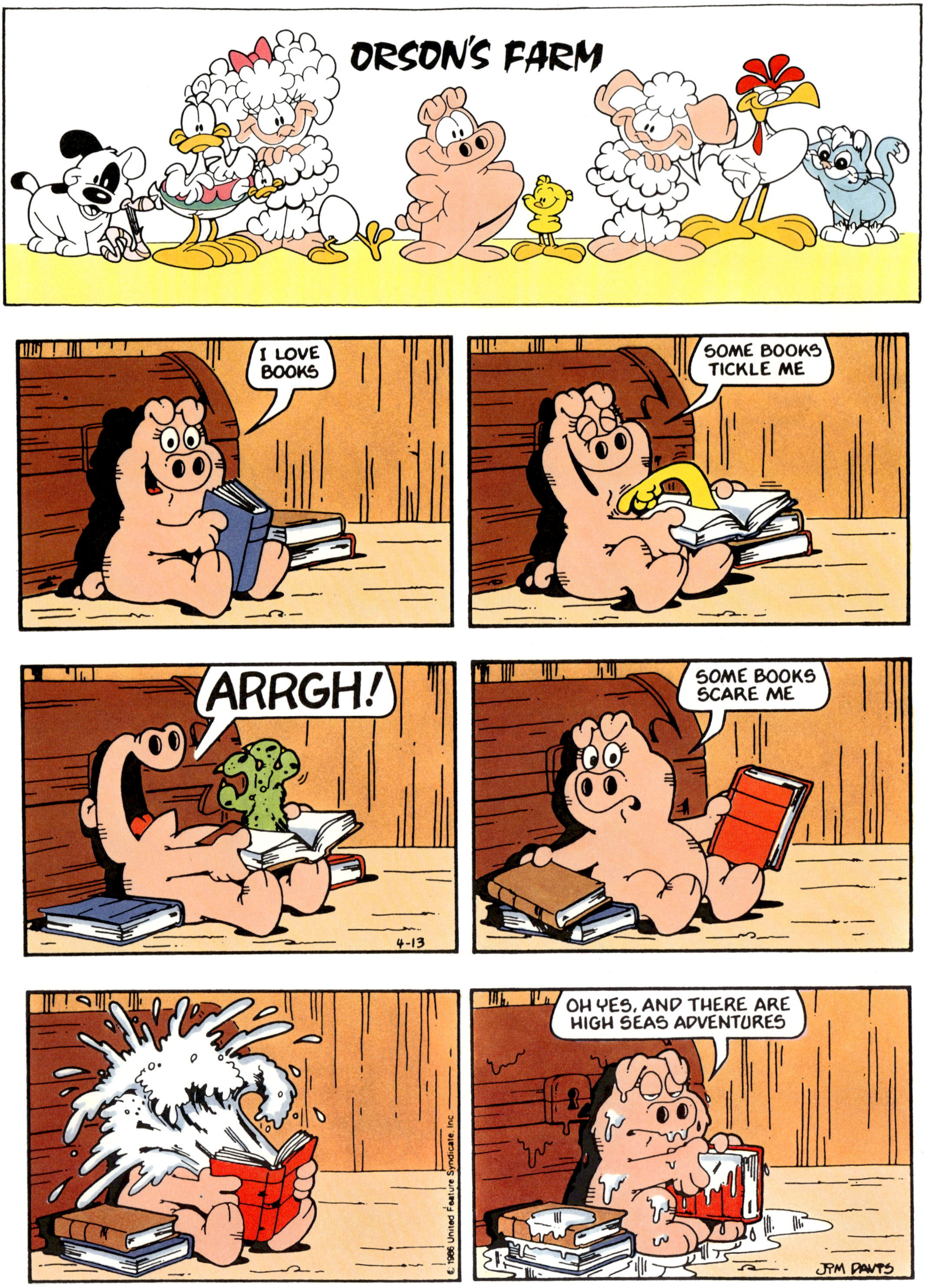

ORSON'S FARM
I LOVE BOOKS
SOME BOOKS TICKLE ME
ARRGH!
4-13
SOME BOOKS SCARE ME
© 1986 United Feature Syndicate, Inc
OH YES, AND THERE ARE HIGH SEAS ADVENTURES
JIM DAVIS

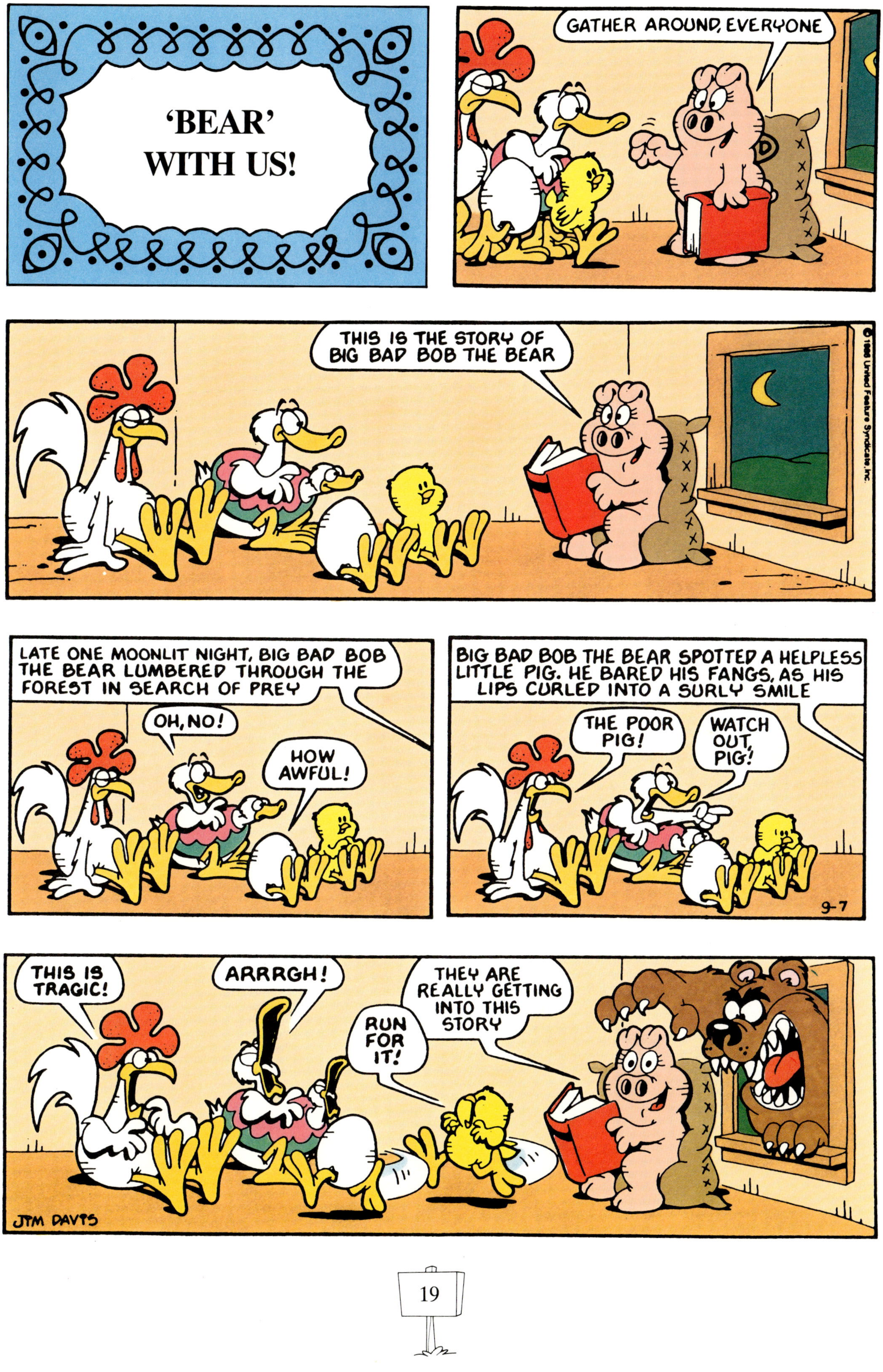
'BEAR' WITH US!
GATHER AROUND, EVERYONE
THIS IS THE STORY OF BIG BAD BOB THE BEAR
© 1986 United Feature Syndicate, Inc.
LATE ONE MOONLIT NIGHT, BIG BAD BOB THE BEAR LUMBERED THROUGH THE FOREST IN SEARCH OF PREY
OH, NO!
HOW AWFUL!
BIG BAD BOB THE BEAR SPOTTED A HELPLESS LITTLE PIG. HE BARED HIS FANGS, AS HIS LIPS CURLED INTO A SURLY SMILE
THE POOR PIG!
WATCH OUT, PIG!
9-7
THIS IS TRAGIC!
ARRRGH!
RUN FOR IT!
THEY ARE REALLY GETTING INTO THIS STORY
JIM DAVIS

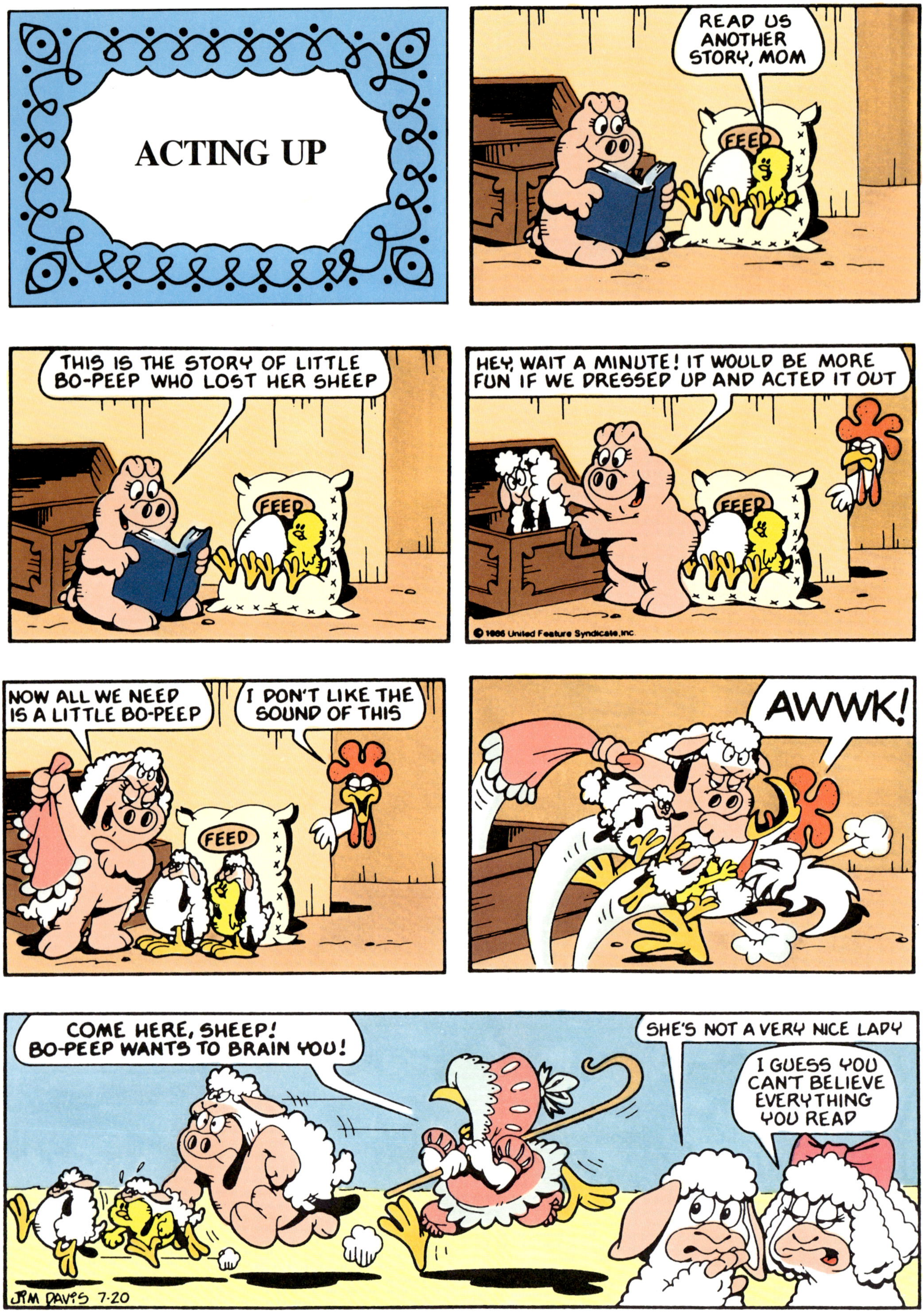
ACTING UP
READ US ANOTHER STORY, MOM
THIS IS THE STORY OF LITTLE BO-PEEP WHO LOST HER SHEEP
HEY, WAIT A MINUTE! IT WOULD BE MORE FUN IF WE DRESSED UP AND ACTED IT OUT
© 1986 United Feature Syndicate, Inc
NOW ALL WE NEED IS A LITTLE BO-PEEP
I DON'T LIKE THE SOUND OF THIS
AWWK!
COME HERE, SHEEP! BO-PEEP WANTS TO BRAIN YOU!
SHE'S NOT A VERY NICE LADY
I GUESS YOU CAN'T BELIEVE EVERYTHING YOU READ
JIM DAVIS 7-20

Bo's Little Lamb Page

A special fun-story for all younger readers. When you see a picture, say what it is out loud.

 WAS FEELING FED-UP. "IT'S 'S BIRTHDAY PARTY TODAY," HE SIGHED, "AND I WANTED TO WEAR MY PARTY HAT – BUT I CAN'T FIND IT ANYWHERE!"  DECIDED TO GO AND LOOK FOR HIS HAT. "MAYBE  HID IT IN THE  FOR A TRICK!" HE EXCLAIMED. THE HAT WAS NOT THERE. "PERHAPS IT BLEW AWAY THE LAST TIME I WORE IT " THOUGHT BO. "IT COULD BE OVER THE  UP THE  OR BEHIND THAT . THE PARTY HAT WAS NOT IN ANY OF THESE PLACES EITHER. "I MUST HAVE PUT IT IN MY  OF DRESSING-UP CLOTHES BY MISTAKE!" DECIDED . THERE WAS A COWBOY HAT, A POLICEMAN'S HAT AND A PIRATE HAT – BUT NO PARTY HAT! "I GIVE UP!" SIGHED . "I JUST WON'T GO, THAT'S ALL!" THEN ALONG CAME . "I SEE YOU'RE READY FOR THE PARTY!" HE CHUCKLED. "WHAT DO YOU MEAN?" EXCLAIMED . "YOU'RE WEARING YOUR PARTY HAT ALREADY!" POINTED . "NO WONDER I COULDN'T FIND IT," LAUGHED . "IT WAS ON MY HEAD ALL THE TIME!"

ROY'S PARTY TRICKS PARADE

Roy, the great practical joker at Orson's Farm, knows lots of funny tricks which he likes to play at parties. Here are some of his favourites for you to try for yourself. They are all harmless, easy to learn and involve little or nothing in the way of equipment. So have fun – and astonish your friends!

First of all, ask a grown-up to break the heads off a dozen or so safety matches and give you the matchsticks to use for tricks.

MATCH THIS!

Place 10 matchsticks on a table and invite a friend to make them into a monkey. He will try to arrange them into a picture and fail. To show him how it's done, arrange the matchsticks so they spell the word APE.

Similarly, you can place 7 matchsticks on the table and ask your friend to take one away and leave none. When he says this is impossible, you arrange six matchsticks to spell the word NIL.

MAGIC MIRROR

Tell your friends that your mirror is magic and invite one of them to prove it by breathing on the glass. When he does this, a spooky message like 'NOW DO YOU BELIEVE ME?' appears! How is this done? Before the party, just write the message on the mirror with your finger. Amazingly, it won't show until someone breathes on the mirror.

THIS ONE'S A SNIP!

Ask a friend if he can cut a square in a piece of paper with only a single snip of the scissors. When he says it can't be done, you fold the paper into quarters and snip off the folded corner in the middle. When you open the paper up, there will be a cut square.

GLASSY EYED

Take an empty glass and place it on the table, upside down. Then put 3 matchsticks beside it and invite one of your friends to put one of the matches on top of it by using the other two. After some difficulty, he will succeed in doing this – but you say: "No, you've failed!" "Why?" he will retort, indignantly. "I asked you to put one of the matches on the top of the glass. You've put it on the BOTTOM!"

MY WORD!

Ask your friend if he can write '100 miles above the ground' in 4 words. When he can't do it, you take the pencil and write:

100 miles
the ground

SHAKE, RATTLE AND ROLL

Put three matchboxes on a table and tell your friends that only one of them contains any matchsticks. Pick up each box in turn and shake it, proving that only one rattles. Then switch the boxes round and invite your friend to point to the box containing the matches. They will be mystified when it's found that all *three* boxes are empty!

How's it done?

You have a fourth matchbox taped inside your left sleeve. This has matchsticks in it which rattle when you shake your arm. Pick up two of the matchboxes from the table with your right arm and one with your left arm. The one you shake with your left arm will sound as it it has matches inside it!

ORSON'S FARM
IT'S MORNING AND TIME TO BLAST THE FARM ANIMALS AWAKE!
MY, MY, DON'T THEY LOOK PEACEFUL?
Z
BLAT!
SHELDON!
GONK
I'M DROWNING?
© 1986 United Feature Syndicate, Inc.
I'LL SAVE YOU!.. WOAH!
LOOK OUT!
ARRGH!
GOSH, I LOVE THIS JOB!
JIM DAVIS 6-29

FRUIT FOOL
Z
BLAT!
WAH-HA!
HA HA HA!
OOO, THAT ROY MAKES ME SO MAD, I'M GOING TO FIX HIM!
THAT NIGHT...
HEE HEE, THE NEXT TIME ROY BLATS HIS BUGLE, HE'LL BLOW A GASKET
Z
THE NEXT MORNING
Z
1986 United Feature Syndicate, Inc.
BLAT!
JIM DAVIS 5-4
WHAT HAPPENED?
I DON'T KNOW WHAT YOU'RE TALKING ABOUT!

BUGLE BOYS
LOOK, SHELDON, ROY'S ASLEEP!
Z
AND THERE'S HIS BUGLE!
LET'S HAVE SOME FUN!
© 1986 United Feature Syndicate, Inc
?
TOOT
BLAT
BLEET
BLAT
TOOT
TOOT
Z
JIM DAVIS 10-26

CODY'S CANINE CROSSWORD

A puzzle all about DOGS.

Across
1. Not a pedigree dog (7)
4. Wild animal closely related to the dog (3)
5. Famous breed of dog – Cocker or Springer — (7)
10. Number of claws on two feet (3)
11. Proper name for sheepdog shows (6)
13. A dog is always loyal to — master (3)
14. Describes a hard or tough dog's coat (4)
16. Dogs pant when they get like this (3)
17. Famous cartoon dog with surname of Bassett (4)
18. A Setter often has this colour coat (3)
19. Dogs love to have a — made of them (4)
21. — wolfhound or — terrier, dogs from the Emerald Isle (5)
22. In town, your dog must wear this to go for a walk (4)

Down
1. Bull —, a big, fierce dog often used to guard buildings (7)
2. A dog will be loyal to its master for — (4)
3. You need one of these to feed your dog (4)
6. Most family dogs are one of these (3)
7. A sheepdog is trained to — every call (6)
9. A dog curls this when it growls (3)
12. Every dog should do this on command (3)
15. Most dogs aren't allowed to chase cats, chew up shoes or lie on the sofa – but they have other —! (5)
16. A dog is the best possible burglar alarm for this place (5)
20. Most dogs seem to have this expressions (3)

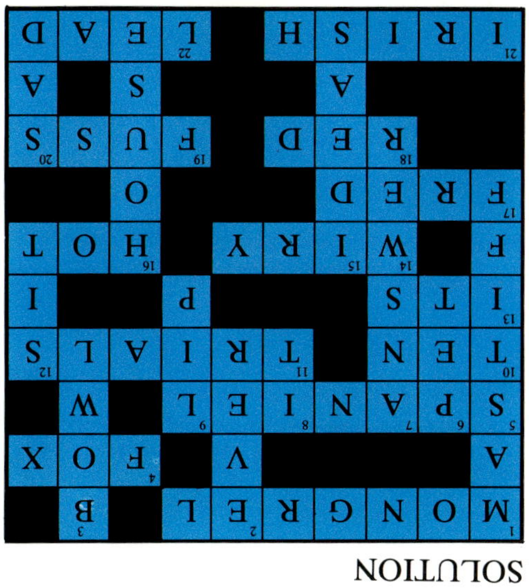

SOLUTION

ORSON'S FARM

CHICKENS ARE SMARTER THAN PIGS
OH YEAH?
YEAH!
© 1986 United Feature Syndicate, Inc.
OH YEAH?!
YEAH!
OH YEAH?!
FEED
JIM DAVIS 10-5
YEAH!
THAT'S CHEATING!

DREAM HOLIDAY
Z
Z
Z
Z
Z
Z
Z
SPLOIT
SPLOIT
SPLOIT
© 1986 United Feature Syndicate, Inc
Z
Z
PLIT
PLIT
PLIT
JIM DAVIS 11-9
SO, HOW WAS YOUR NIGHT, ORSON?
I DREAMED I WENT TO THE SOUTH OF FRANCE FOR A HOLIDAY. I STOOD ON THE BEACH AND GAZED UPON THE BEAUTIFUL BLUE MEDITERRANEAN...
AND THEN I DRANK IT

FLOWER POWER
COME ALONG, CHILDREN, LET'S WATER THE FLOWERS
EVEN FLOWERS NEED A DRINK OF WATER NOW AND THEN
FLOWERS NEED A GOOD STOMPING TOO
TIPTOE THROUGH THE TULIPS!
STOP THAT, ROY! VINNY ISN'T GOING TO LIKE THAT!
WHO'S VINNY?
MY VENUS FLYTRAP
© 1986 United Feature Syndicate, Inc.
JIM DAVIS 7-13

BEWARE OF THE DUCK

It was nap time. Orson was telling a scary story about vampires. "Count Dracula descended from his coach in his long, black cloak," whispered Orson. "He smiled at the simple peasant girl who was gathering flowers by the roadside."

Inside the barn Lanolin, Bo, Sheldon and Booker sat open-mouthed with fear as the story unfolded. But they were not the only ones who were listening. Outside the window, Wade was also hanging onto every word. He had been pecking up corn in the farmyard when Orson's voice reached his ears. Now he was hooked on the story too.

"Count Dracula offered to help the peasant girl with her task," continued Orson. "'How kind of you, sir,' she replied." "Hey!" interrupted Sheldon. "Why didn't she run away? "Because," explained Orson, dropping his voice to a sinister whisper, "there was no way of telling that Dracula was a vampire except that he had no shadow!"

Outside in the yard, Wade made a mental note to check that everyone he met from now on had a shadow. Then he looked down at the ground and he began to tremble with terror. "I have no shadow!" he gasped. "I m-m-must be a vampire!"

Wade wandered off in a daze. "Me, a vampire?" he thought. "It can't be true!" Yet whenever he looked behind him, there was no trace of a shadow on the ground. He decided to ask some of his friends if he was a vampire. "Er, excuse me, Roy," he said, tapping the rooster on the shoulder. "HELLO, Wade!" replied Roy. Wade was nearly bowled over backwards by the smell of garlic! "Vampires are afraid of garlic!" thought Wade, quickly. "Roy's been eating it to keep me at bay." So Wade fled, yelling. "I'll never understand that duck!" muttered Roy.

Then Wade spotted Blue polishing a mirror outside the farmhouse. "Er, excuse me, Blue . . ." he began, and then stopped. When Wade looked in the mirror, he could not see himself! "Vampires have no reflection," he gulped, "so I *am* one! WAAHAAAGHHH!" Wade fled again. "What a strange person that duck is!" agreed Blue.

Wade scampered round the corner of the barn and collided with Orson who was just coming out after storytime. "D-D-Don't speak to me," spluttered Wade, "I might bite you!" "Really?" exclaimed Orson. "Yes, really!" repeated Wade. "You see, I'm a vampire." "YOU? A vampire?" guffawed Orson. And he rolled on the ground, clutching his sides with mirth. Wade looked down at him, rather crossly. "Of course I'm a vampire!" he snapped. And he explained about the mirror. "That's not a mirror!" cried Orson, getting to his feet. "That's a window. Blue's promised to clean them for the farmer in return for being taken for a walk every day." "But what about the garlic?" queried Wade. "Didn't you know?" laughed Orson. "Roy likes eating Italian food which is full of garlic." Then Wade mentioned the missing shadow. Orson rolled on the ground again. "What's so funny about that?" snorted Wade. "If I wasn't a vampire, I'd have a shadow." "The reason you don't have a shadow, Wade," grinned Orson, "is that there's no sun. It's night-time!"

A wave of relief swept over Wade. "So I'm NOT a vampire!" he exclaimed. "Now I can go home and sleep easy in my bed!"

Wade did just that. He found himself a comfy pillow, lay back with his hands behind his head and drifted off to sleep. He dreamt he was in a beautiful land made entirely of marshmallows.

Then midnight struck. The moon, which so far had been hidden by a thick bank of cloud, suddenly appeared. It was a full moon, round and yellow. And somewhere in the distance, a coyote began to howl. Wade, in his dream, began eating the marshmallows. As he dreamt, the sleeping duck began pecking at his pillow. Slowly, it split open and the horsehair inside began to spill out.

Wade woke up. He felt itchy and tingling all over. Looking up, he saw the full moon and heard the distant howling. Then he looked down and saw that he was covered in coarse brown hair. His blood turned to ice. "WAAHAAGHHH!" he yelled. "Now I've turned into a W-W-WEREWOLF!"

Wade ran round and round the farmyard, yelling. 'I'm a werewolf! I'm a werewolf!" His screaming woke the other animals. "Is Wade *really* a werewolf?" Booker asked Orson. "No," replied Orson, shaking his head, "but he is definitely one crazy duck!"

ORSON'S FARM

HEY, WADE. LET'S GO SWIMMING
SWIMMING?!
© 1986 United Feature Syndicate, Inc.
NO WAY! I'M AFRAID OF WATER
YOU DON'T HAVE TO GET INTO THE WATER. JUST STAND NEXT TO IT
I DON'T?
NO. WE WANT YOU TO COME WITH US. WE NEED YOU
HOW NICE! THEY NEED ME
JIM DAVIS 8-24
DOING

TAKING THE PLUNGE
WADE, COME OVER HERE
NAH. TRUST ME
HEY, WADE, WHY DON'T YOU GO FOR A SWIM?
NO WAY! I'D SINK!
YOU CAN'T SINK. YOU'RE WEARING AN INNER TUBE
I CAN'T?
SPLASH
I HATE HIM
United Feature Syndicate, Inc.
JIM DAVIS 11-2

DUCKING OUT
HEY, LET'S GIVE WADE A SWIMMING LESSON
HOW ARE WE SUPPOSED TO TEACH WADE HOW TO SWIM?
SIMPLE. JUST DO WHAT I DO, ROY
JIM DAVIS 8-17
HEY, WADE, YOU'RE GOING TO LEARN TO SWIM TODAY
1986 United Feature Syndicate, Inc.
NO WAY! I'M AFRAID OF WATER!
DON'T WORRY ABOUT A THING
WE'LL BE WITH YOU ALL THE TIME!
ARRRRGH!
ANY MORE BRIGHT IDEAS, ORSON?
HOW COULD I KNOW DUCKS RUN ON WATER?

Wade's Watery Maze

Poor Wade! He was wandering around the farmyard, feeling quite calm for once, when his rubber ring caught on a thorn. WHOOSH! Wade found himself being jet-propelled through the air and landed with a bump some distance away. A passing cyclist kindly mended the hole with his puncture-repair kit, but now Wade has to make his way back and – terror of terrors – he has to cross lots of WATER!

Can you help Wade to find a way through the watery obstacles back to Orson's Farm?

Colouring Picture

You can colour this delightful picture of life down on the farm with your paints, felt-tips or crayons.

ORSON'S FARM
BARNYARDS ARE MORE FUN THAN PLAYGROUNDS
WHO NEEDS SWINGS?
WHO NEEDS SLIDES?
WHO NEEDS MONKEY BARS?
JIM DAVIS 4-6
© 1988 United Feature Syndicate, Inc.
I THINK I'LL STICK TO THE TEETER-TOTTER

STICK-IN-THE-MUDS
I HATE RAINY DAYS. THERE'S NOTHING TO DO
YES THERE IS, ROY, MUD SLIDE!
WHEEE!
HEY, THAT LOOKS LIKE FUN!
© 1986 United Feature Syndicate Inc
YAHOOOO!!
OH NO! THE SUN'S COMING OUT! QUICK! TO THE PUMP TO WASH OFF!
TOO LATE
ANOTHER BRILLIANT IDEA, ORSON
WHAT DO WE DO NOW?
MAYBE IT'LL RAIN AGAIN
JIM DAVIS 1-6

THE TRACTOR FACTOR

Sheldon's Spot the Difference

There are 10 differences between these two pictures of Sheldon holding a balloon. Can you spot them?

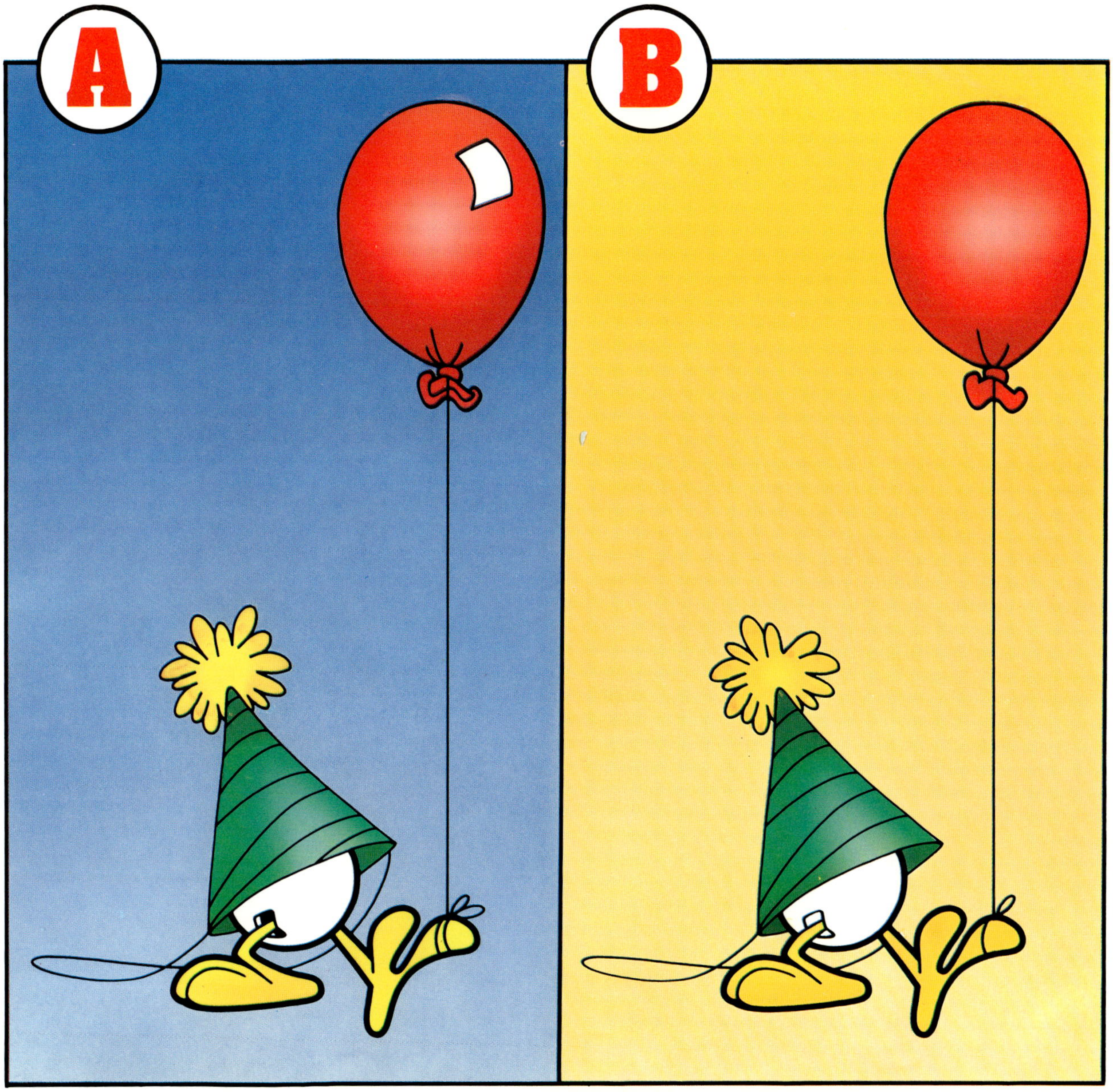

Answers

From left to right, the following items are missing from picture B:

1. One of the points of the pom-pom
2. The very top stripe of the hat
3. The shadow around the top of Sheldon's leg
4. The very bottom stripe of the hat
5. The length of string above Sheldon's upturned foot
6. One of the pieces of string around Sheldon's foot
7. One loop of the bow just above his foot.
8. The inner fold of the balloon nozzle
9. One of the three curve lines above the nozzle
10. The square of shadow at top of balloon.

ORSON'S FARM
CHUG CHUG
COWBOY ROY MOUNTS A WILD BRONCO!
JIM DAVIS
10-12
YEE-HAH!
© 1986 United Feature Syndicate Inc
COWBOY ROY WINS THE RODEO!
POOMP
POOMP
SPACE ACE ORSON AND HIS FRIENDS LAND SAFELY ON THE PLANET CLARION!

POOL PARTY

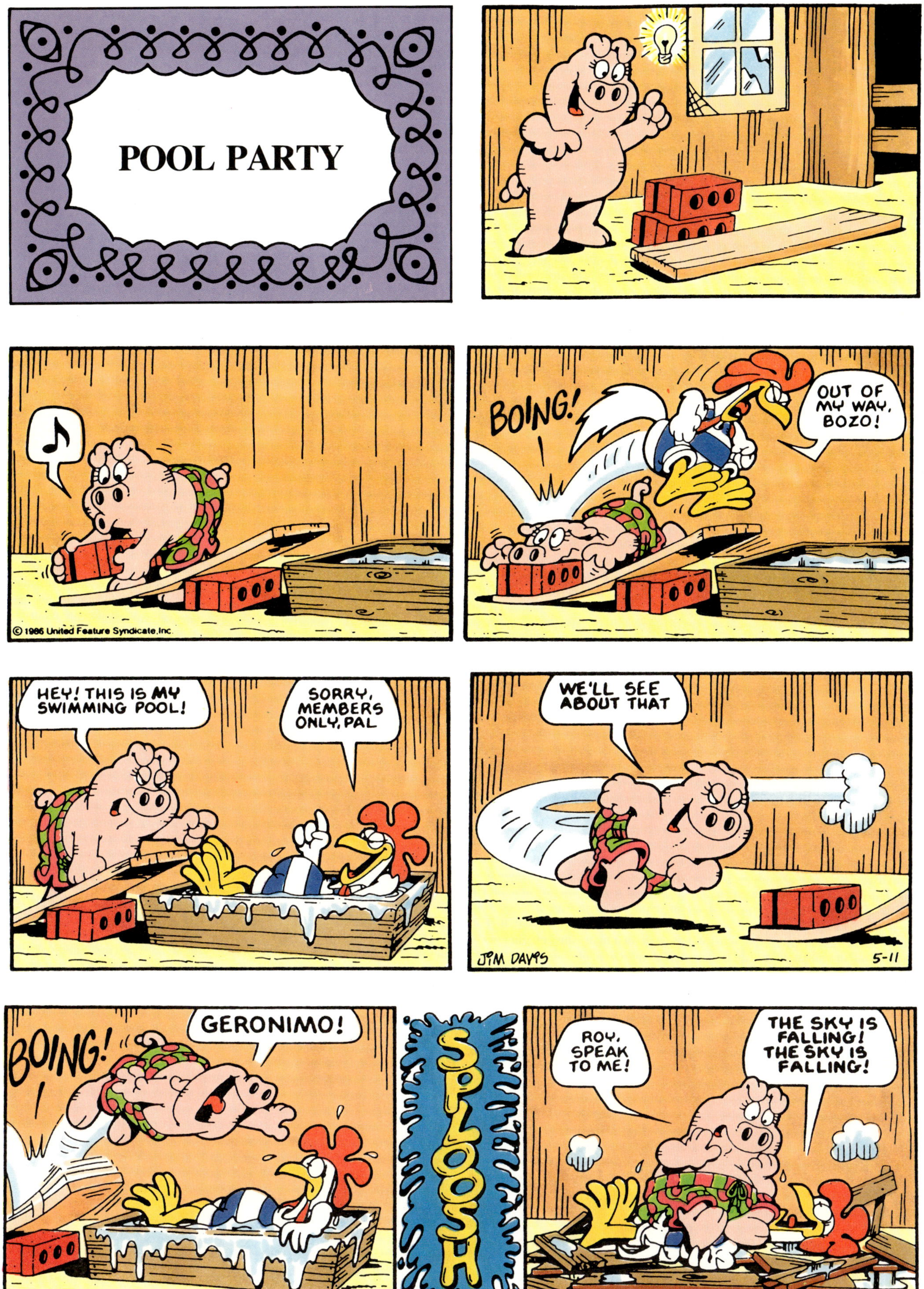

BOING!
OUT OF MY WAY, BOZO!
© 1986 United Feature Syndicate, Inc.
HEY! THIS IS MY SWIMMING POOL!
SORRY, MEMBERS ONLY, PAL
WE'LL SEE ABOUT THAT
JIM DAVIS
5-11
BOING!
GERONIMO!
SPLOOSH
ROY, SPEAK TO ME!
THE SKY IS FALLING! THE SKY IS FALLING!

SPRINGBOARD TO SUCCESS

BOOKER'S Farmyard Wordsearch

Here are 20 words connected with farms and farming. Can you find them in the grid? (The words are spelt in all directions – forwards, backwards, up, down and diagonally!)

Fertilizer
Potatoes
Haystack
Cows
Pond
Straw
Tractor
Pigs
Cat
Wheat
Turkey
Stubble
Horse
Hen
Geese
Silage
Barley
Plough
Rabbit
Corn

E	C	O	R	N	T	A	E	H	W	T
S	N	H	G	U	O	L	P	Z	S	T
E	F	E	R	T	I	L	I	Z	E	R
E	C	K	H	S	G	I	P	H	B	A
G	E	O	P	A	A	Z	O	O	A	C
Y	B	O	W	W	Y	T	T	S	R	T
B	N	T	A	S	I	S	A	R	L	O
D	Y	R	Y	B	Y	Y	T	E	E	R
S	T	U	B	B	L	E	O	A	Y	L
S	O	A	C	A	T	M	E	Z	C	L
L	R	E	G	A	L	I	S	X	W	K

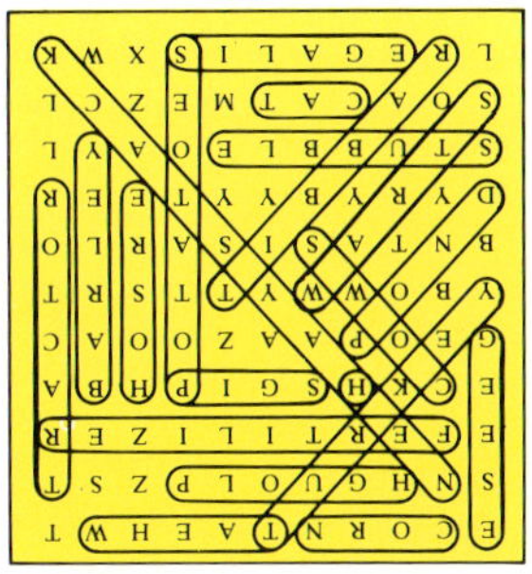

SOLUTION

YOU CAN'T BEAT A TV SNACK

ORSON'S FARM
WAKE UP, EVERYBODY! THE CHRISTMAS SEASON IS HERE!
ALL RIGHT!
DECORATIONS! WE NEED DECORATIONS!
JIM DAVIS
12-21
SOMETHING IS MISSING
YOU BEAN BRAINS. YOU NEED A CHRISTMAS TREE
A WHAT?
© 1986 United Feature Syndicate, Inc.
YOU KNOW, A CHRISTMAS TREE. IT'S ABOUT THIS HIGH AND THIS WIDE
DON'T MOVE, ROY
IS THIS SOME KIND OF JOKE?
HOLD STILL WHILE I PLUG YOU IN

DEEP TROUBLE
PAT PAT PAT
SPLAT
© 1986 United Feature Syndicate, Inc.
HAR HAR HAR HAR!
HA HA HA
WHAP WHAP WHAP
BOY, DO YOU LOOK STUPID!
JIM DAVIS 12-28
WUMP
I MEANT TO DO THAT!

DOWNHILL ALL THE WAY
THIS LOOKS LIKE A GOOD HILL
READY, KIDS?
READY!!
THEN LET'S PUSH OFF
© 1986 United Feature Syndicate, Inc.
WHEEEEE!
BOOF
JIM DAVIS 12-7

BLUE'S FELINE FITWORD

A puzzle all about CATS

Can you fit these words into the grid?
(You'll find it easier if you use the long words first.)

(3) mew	(4) milk	(5) moggy	(6) catnap	(7) mongrel	(8) whiskers
lap	tail	lions		purring	
	eyes			Burmese	
	puss				

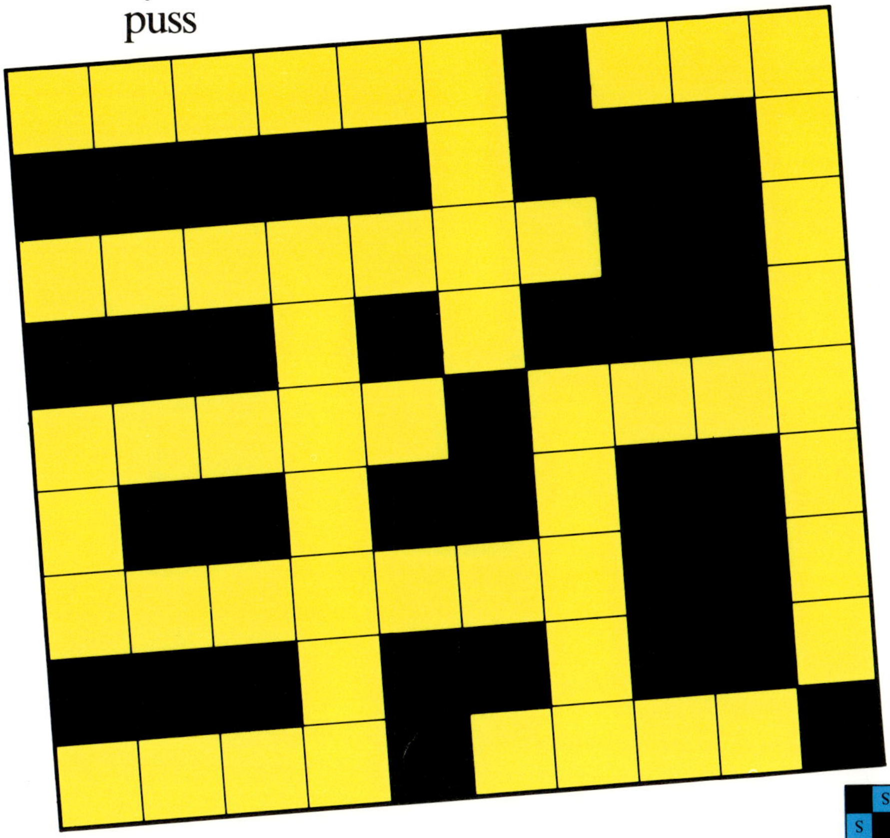

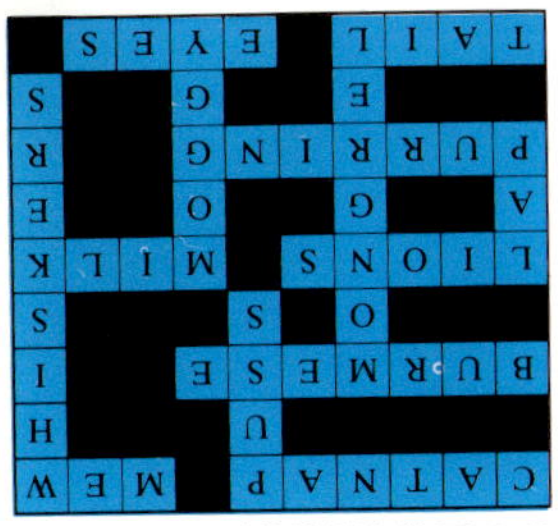

SOLUTION

Worm's Underground Quiz

Worm lives underground with his wife and son, Little Willie. They like their cosy, subterranean home which has all mod-cons and provides a safe hidey-hole from the attentions of Booker. In fact, the Worms are not alone in enjoying their underground lifestyle. A number of other animals, plants and interesting man-made objects can be found down there too. So here are 10 questions about the fascinating world beneath our feet.

1. What is the proper name for the maze of underground tunnels and chambers dug by rabbits.

2. What was the first city in the world to have an Underground Railway?
(a) Paris
(b) London
(c) New York

3. Can you complete this sentence?
'An ARCHAEOLOGIST is a person who studies — — — — — — — by digging up objects from the ground.' (2 words)

4. Which of these vegetables does NOT grow underground?
(a) Potato
(b) Carrot
(c) Parsnip
(d) Cauliflower
(e) Turnip

5. The badger is another famous underground animal. What is the correct name for:
(a) A male badger?
(b) A badger's home?

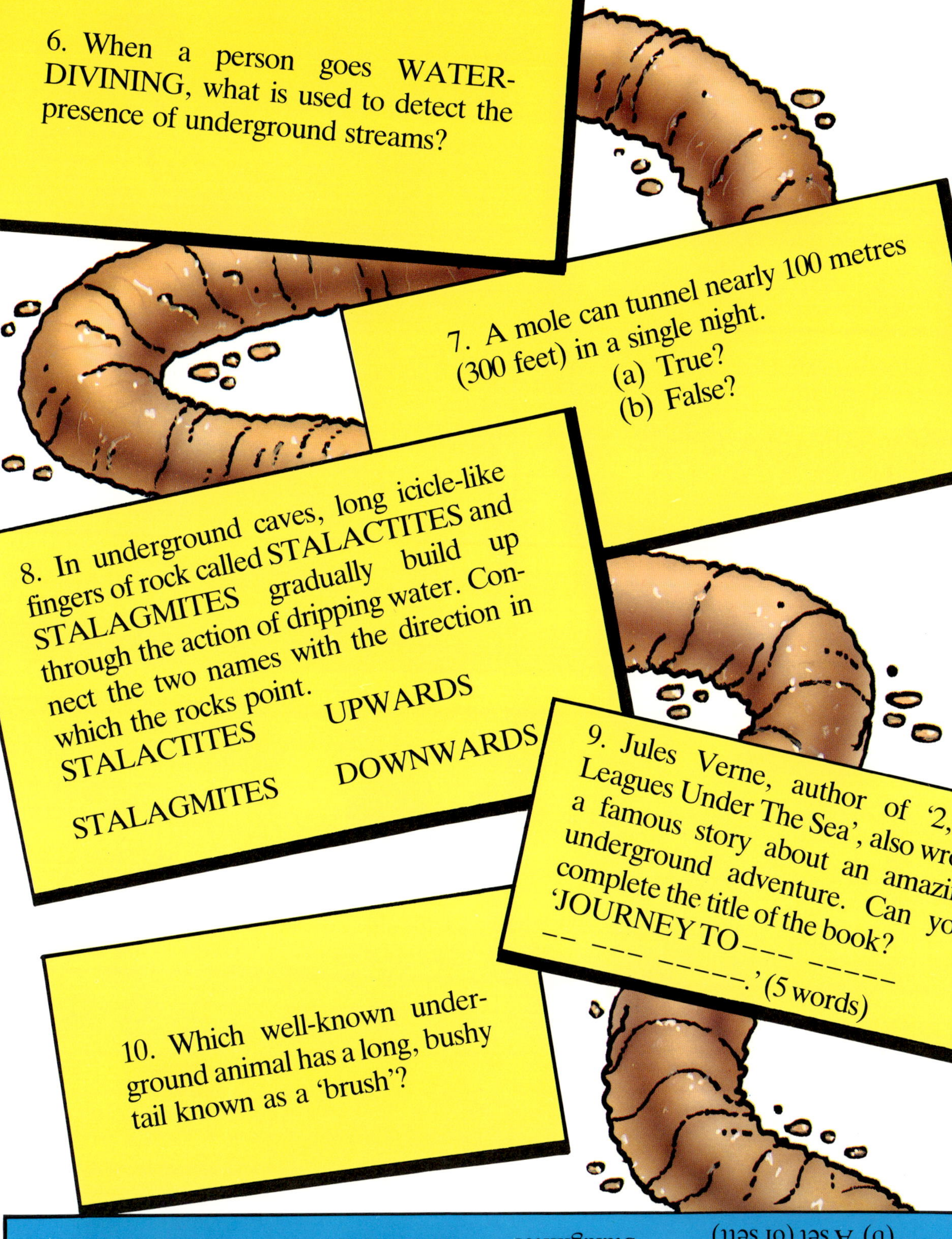

6. When a person goes WATER-DIVINING, what is used to detect the presence of underground streams?

7. A mole can tunnel nearly 100 metres (300 feet) in a single night.
(a) True?
(b) False?

8. In underground caves, long icicle-like fingers of rock called STALACTITES and STALAGMITES gradually build up through the action of dripping water. Connect the two names with the direction in which the rocks point.

STALACTITES	UPWARDS
STALAGMITES	DOWNWARDS

9. Jules Verne, author of '2,000 Leagues Under The Sea', also wrote a famous story about an amazing underground adventure. Can you complete the title of the book? 'JOURNEY TO--- ----- -- --- -----.' (5 words)

10. Which well-known underground animal has a long, bushy tail known as a 'brush'?

Answers

1. A warren
2. (b) London
3. The Past
4. (d) Cauliflower
5. (a) A boar
   (b) A set (or sett)
6. A thin stick, usually shaped like the letter Y
7. (a) True
8. Stalactites ✕ upwards
   Stalagmites ✕ downwards
   (Stalactites – downwards; Stalagmites – upwards)
9. The Centre Of The Earth
10. The fox

ORSON'S FARM
ZIP
ALL RIGHT, WORM! NO MORE FOOLING AROUND! I'M COMING IN AFTER YOU!
© 1986 United Feature Syndicate, Inc
THOOMP
UH-OH
BOOKER, ARE YOU STUCK?
YES, ROY. DO SOMETHING!
KITCHEY, KITCHEY, KITCHEY
ROY!
JIM DAVIS 11-30

THE BITER BIT
© 1986 United Feature Syndicate, Inc
BOOKER, WHAT ARE YOU DOING?
FISHING FOR WORMS
FISHING FOR WORMS. HOW CUTE
AND WHAT ARE YOU USING FOR BAIT?
JIM DAVIS 11-23

APPLIANCE OF SCIENCE
© 1986 United Feature Syndicate, Inc
JIM DAVIS 6-8
TRY THIS BUCKET, MOM
GOOD IDEA!

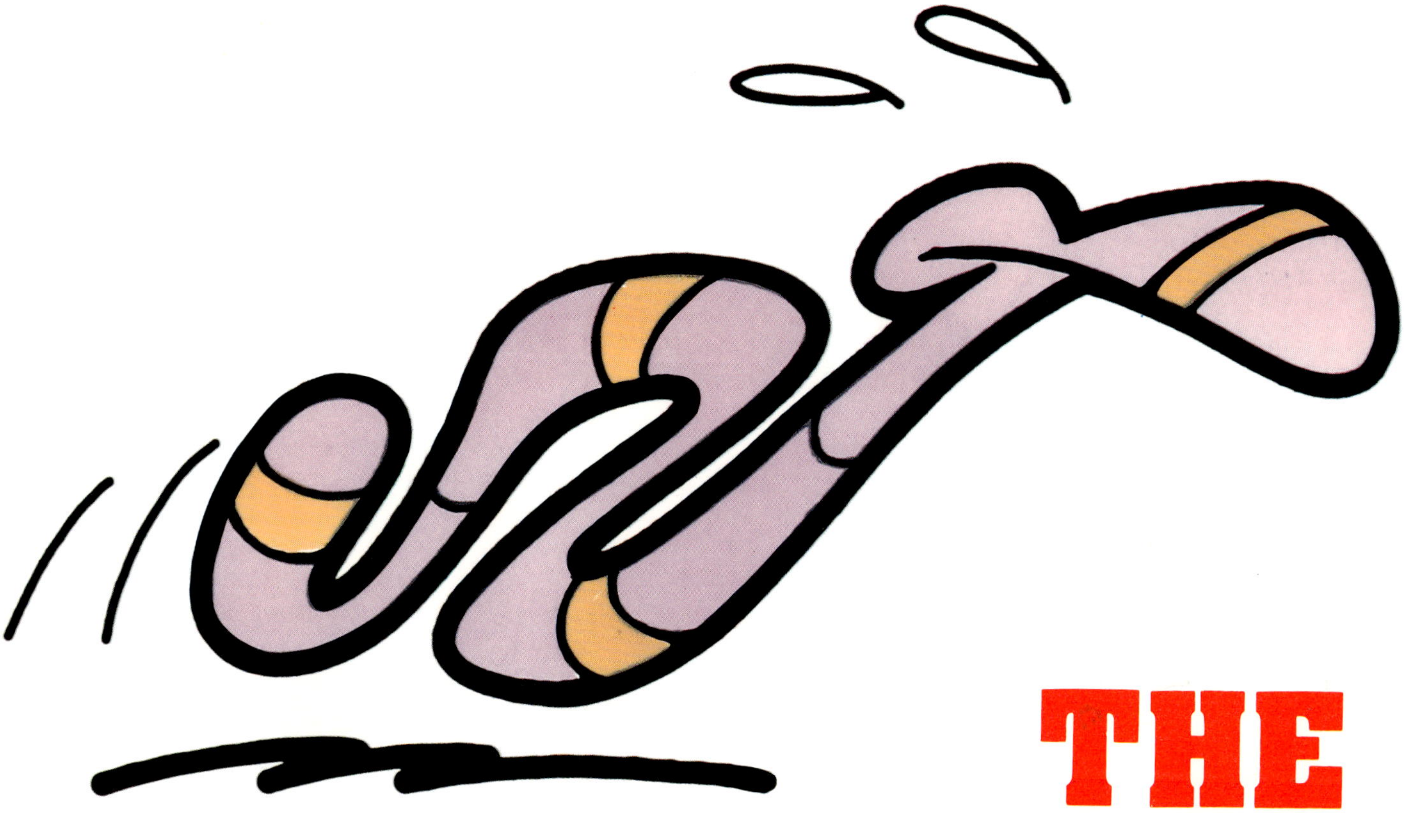

THE WORM HAS TURNED

"Will I get away this time?" gasped Worm, wriggling frantically across the fields. "If I don't, it's curtains for me!" It was a warm Spring day and Worm had grown tired of his dark, underground home. Emerging from his hole into the bright sunshine, he had wandered further than usual around the farm and had sat down to sunbathe beside a rock. Suddenly, Booker had surprised him and now the chick was in hot pursuit, gaining with every stride. "My hole doesn't seem to be getting any nearer," puffed Worm, "I d-d-don't think I'm going to make it!"

Worm *did* make it – but only just! He slithered down his hole just as Booker's beak snapped together millimetres above his tail. "I'll get you next time, Worm!" yelled Booker. "Just you wait and see!" "He could be right, dear!" said Mrs Worm, looking up from her knitting. "Yes, Dad," agreed Little Willie, "you're not getting any younger, are you?"

When Worm had recovered his breath, he thought about what his family had said. "Maybe I *do* take a few chances now and then," he agreed, "and so far I've managed to get away with it. One day, though, I suppose I could come unstuck!" Worm began to imagine what life would be like if he were not always at war with Booker. "It would be wonderful!" he concluded. "No more worry, fear or panic. And we Worms could go above ground whenever we wanted. The wife's never seen round the farmyard."

So Worm decided it was time to call a truce!

Meanwhile, back at the barn, Booker was hobbling painfully towards Orson. "Don't tell me you've sprained your foot again?" exclaimed Orson. "Afraid so, Mom, sighed Booker, "And I suppose you did this chasing after Worm?" added Orson. "Afraid so, Mom," repeated Booker. "Well, serves you right!" concluded Orson. "If you spend all your time trying to catch Worm, you've got to expect to get hurt." "You're right, Mom," agreed Booker, "I'll stop."

The following morning, Booker approached Worm's hole with a jaunty step instead of the usual threatening creep. At the same moment, Worm popped his head out of the hole, waving a little white flag. "Does this mean you want to make friends?" asked Booker. "It certainly does!" replied Worm. "How about it?" "You're on!" agreed Booker.

So the war ended and the peace began. At first, it made a welcome change. Worm was able to spend more time with his family and took Little Willie fishing at an underground stream. Meanwhile, Booker had more time to play with Sheldon and to help Orson with his chores. Then the trouble began . . .

It was about one week later. Worm sat in his armchair, reading the paper. "I'm bored!" he sighed. "I've read this through twice already and it's still only ten o'clock. What am I going to do for the rest of the day?" Worm got up and wandered into the kitchen looking for something to eat. "You're not getting anything," scolded his wife. "You do nothing but eat nowadays. Take Little Willie fishing again if you want something to do!" Willie, however, was watching TV and did not want to go fishing. "Maybe tomorrow, Dad!" he called. "Tomorrow's no good for me," thought Worm, "I need something to do NOW!" Then an idea popped into Worm's head and a big grin spread all over his face.

Worm poked his head out of his hole and called to Booker. "This is for you, beak-features!" he yelled, blowing the biggest raspberry ever heard around Orson's Farm.

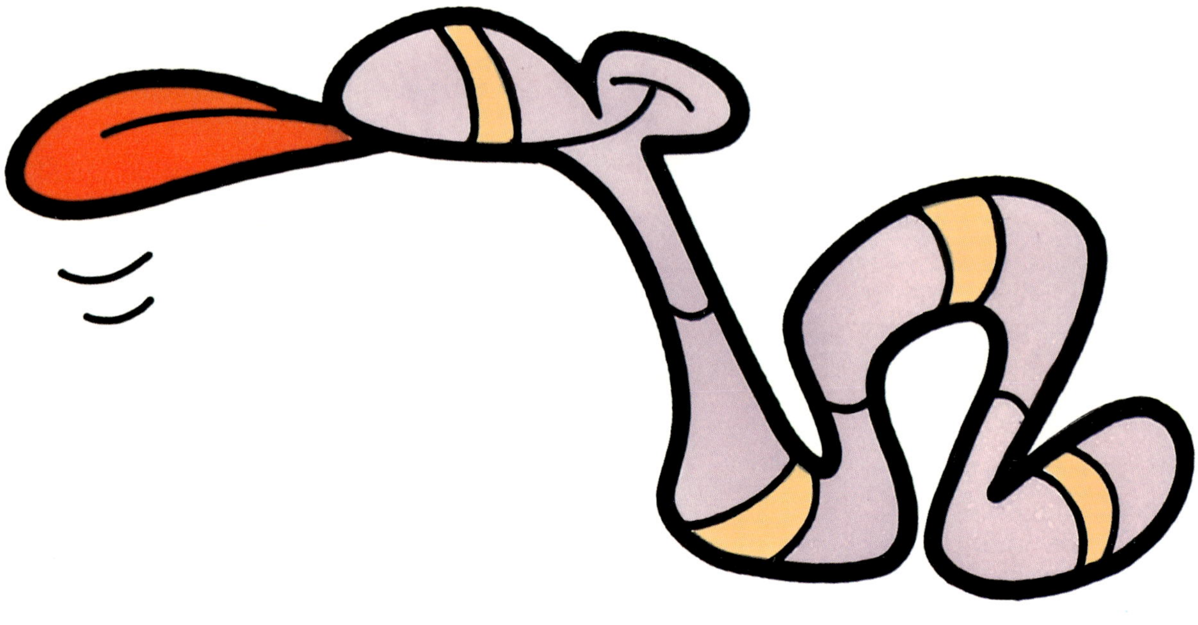

Booker, who had been sent for a walk round the farmyard for getting under Orson's feet, responded with a grin. "Nice one, Worm!" he called. "I'm not joking, chicken-chops," retorted Worm, "this is what I think of you!" And he blew another even bigger raspberry. The smile faded from Booker's face and a frown clouded his brow. "I thought we declared a truce . . ." he began. "Well, you thought wrong didn't you, fluff-pants!" interrupted Worm. "War's declared again from this moment on!"

To prove his point, Worm emerged from his hole and wriggled invitingly towards Booker, sticking his tongue out all the way. Booker needed no second invitation. He had also been at a loose end since the truce and was longing for some action too! "Okay, slither-nose," he yelled, charging forwards, "you've asked for it!" Worm turned and fled with Booker close behind him in irate pursuit. They chased all round the farmyard until Worm just escaped down his hole. "Whatever's going on?" cried Mrs Worm, coming in from the kitchen. "Oh, nothing dear," grinned Worm, "just business as usual!"

FEED